United States Government Accountability Office

GAO

Report to the Subcommittee on Federal Financial Management, Government Information, Federal Services, and International Security, Committee on Homeland Security and Governmental Affairs United States Senate

July 2012

||||||||| I0425851

SOFTWARE DEVELOPMENT

Effective Practices and Federal Challenges in Applying Agile Methods

GAO
Accountability ★ Integrity ★ Reliability

GAO-12-681

G A O
Accountability * Integrity * Reliability
Highlights

Highlights of GAO-12-681, a report to the Subcommittee on Federal Financial Management, Government Information, Federal Services, and International Security, Committee on Homeland Security and Governmental Affairs, United States Senate

SOFTWARE DEVELOPMENT

Effective Practices and Federal Challenges in Applying Agile Methods

Why GAO Did This Study

Federal agencies depend on IT to support their missions and spent at least $76 billion on IT in fiscal year 2011. However, long-standing congressional interest has contributed to the identification of numerous examples of lengthy IT projects that incurred cost overruns and schedule delays while contributing little to mission-related outcomes. To reduce the risk of such problems, the Office of Management and Budget (OMB) recommends modular software delivery consistent with an approach known as Agile, which calls for producing software in small, short increments. Recently, several agencies have applied Agile practices to their software projects.

Accordingly, GAO was asked to identify (1) effective practices in applying Agile for software development solutions and (2) federal challenges in implementing Agile development techniques. To do so, GAO identified and interviewed ten experienced users and officials from five federal projects that used Agile methods and analyzed and categorized their responses.

What GAO Recommends

GAO is recommending that the Federal CIO Council, working with its chair, OMB's Deputy Director for Management, include practices such as those discussed in this report in the Council's ongoing effort to promote modular development. After reviewing a draft of this report, OMB commented that the recommendation was better addressed to the Council than to its chair. GAO revised the recommendation to address it to the Council working with its chair.

View GAO-12-681. For more information, contact David A. Powner at (202) 512-9286 or pownerd@gao.gov.

What GAO Found

GAO identified 32 practices and approaches as effective for applying Agile software development methods to IT projects. The practices generally align with five key software development project management activities: strategic planning, organizational commitment and collaboration, preparation, execution, and evaluation. Officials who have used Agile methods on federal projects generally agreed that these practices are effective. Specifically, each practice was used and found effective by officials from at least one agency, and ten practices were used and found effective by officials from all five agencies. The ten practices are

- Start with Agile guidance and an Agile adoption strategy.
- Enhance migration to Agile concepts using Agile terms, such as *user stories* (used to convey requirements), and Agile examples, such as demonstrating how to write a user story.
- Continuously improve Agile adoption at both the project level and organization level.
- Seek to identify and address impediments at the organization and project levels.
- Obtain stakeholder/customer feedback frequently.
- Empower small, cross-functional teams.
- Include requirements related to security and progress monitoring in your queue of unfinished work (the backlog).
- Gain trust by demonstrating value at the end of each iteration.
- Track progress using tools and metrics.
- Track progress daily and visibly.

GAO identified 14 challenges with adapting and applying Agile in the federal environment (see table).

Table: Federal Challenges

Teams had difficulty collaborating closely.	Procurement practices may not support Agile projects.
Teams had difficulty transitioning to self-directed work.	Customers did not trust iterative solutions.
Staff had difficulty committing to more timely and frequent input.	Teams had difficulty managing iterative requirements.
Agencies had trouble committing staff.	Compliance reviews were difficult to execute within an iteration time frame.
Timely adoption of new tools was difficult.	Federal reporting practices do not align with Agile.
Technical environments were difficult to establish and maintain.	Traditional artifact reviews do not align with Agile.
Agile guidance was not clear.	Traditional status tracking does not align with Agile.

Source: GAO.

Finally, officials described efforts to address challenges by clarifying previously unclear guidance on using Agile. In a related effort, the Federal Chief Information Officers (CIO) Council is developing guidance on modular development in the federal government, but it does not specifically address effective practices for Agile.

Contents

Letter		1
	Background	3
	Effective Practices for Applying Agile	9
	Federal Challenges in Applying Agile	15
	Conclusions	21
	Recommendation for Executive Action	22
	Agency Comments and Our Evaluation	22

Appendix I	Objectives, Scope, and Methodology	24

Appendix II	The Agile Manifesto and Principles	26

Appendix III	Experienced Users	28

Appendix IV	Federal Project Profiles	29

Appendix V	Comments from the Department of Veterans Affairs	31

Appendix VI	Comments from the Department of Commerce	33

Appendix VII	GAO Contacts and Staff Acknowledgments	34

Tables

Table 1: Practices Used and Found Effective by Five Agencies	14
Table 2: Profile of Global Combat Support System-J Increment 7	29
Table 3: Profile of National Aeronautics and Space Administration Enterprise Applications Competency Center Materials Management Initiative	29
Table 4: Profile of Patents End-to-End	29
Table 5: Profile of Occupational Health Record-keeping System	30

Table 6: Profile of Affordable Care Act Branded Prescription Drugs   30

Figure

Figure 1: Comparison of Agile and Waterfall Development   7

Abbreviations

CIO	Chief Information Officer
EVM	earned value management
IT	information technology
NASA	National Aeronautics and Space Administration
OMB	Office of Management and Budget
XP	eXtreme Programming

July 27, 2012

The Honorable Thomas R. Carper
Chairman
The Honorable Scott P. Brown
Ranking Member
Subcommittee on Federal Financial Management,
Government Information, Federal Services,
    and International Security
Committee on Homeland Security
    and Governmental Affairs
United States Senate

Information systems are integral to many aspects of federal government operations. To support agency missions, the federal government spent at least $76 billion in fiscal year 2011 on information technology (IT). However, as we have previously reported, prior IT expenditures too often have produced disappointing results, including multimillion dollar cost overruns and schedule delays measured in years, with questionable mission-related achievements.[1] Congress has expressed long-standing interest in monitoring and improving federal IT investments, which have often been developed in long, sequential phases. Recently, several agencies have tried an alternate approach known as Agile, which calls for producing software in small, short increments.

Shorter, more incremental approaches to IT development have been identified as having the potential to improve the way in which the federal government develops and implements IT. For example, the Office of Management and Budget (OMB) recently issued guidance that advocates the use of shorter delivery time frames, an approach consistent with Agile.[2] As federal interest in Agile grows, it is helpful to know how experienced users effectively follow this approach and what challenges it presents in the federal environment.

---

[1]GAO, *Information Management and Technology,* GAO/HR-97-9 (Washington, D.C.: February 1997) and *Information Technology: Critical Factors Underlying Successful Major Acquisitions,* GAO-12-7 (Washington, D.C.: Oct. 21, 2011).

[2]OMB, *25 Point Implementation Plan to Reform Federal Information Technology Management,* (Washington, D.C.: Dec. 9, 2010) and *Immediate Review of Financial Systems IT Projects,* M-10-26 (Washington, D.C.: June 28, 2010).

Accordingly, the objectives of our review were to identify (1) effective practices in applying Agile for software development solutions and (2) federal challenges in implementing Agile development techniques.

To identify effective practices in applying Agile for software development solutions, we interviewed a nongeneralizable sample of experienced Agile users (see app. III).[3] We identified those users from publications, forums, and recommendations from federal and private officials knowledgeable about Agile. To ensure a broad range of experiences, we chose individuals from private, public, and non-profit backgrounds. We asked them individually to describe what they have found to be effective practices in applying Agile methods. We compiled the practices and asked the users to rate them for effectiveness. We then asked officials from a nongeneralizable sample of five federal software development projects that had used Agile methods for their views on the effectiveness of the practices. The projects were selected to reflect a range of agencies, system descriptions, and cost. The five federal agencies supporting these projects were the Departments of Commerce, Defense, and Veterans Affairs, the Internal Revenue Service, and the National Aeronautics and Space Administration (see app. IV for additional information on the projects and responsible officials).

To identify federal challenges in implementing Agile development techniques, we asked the officials from the five projects to identify challenges applying Agile in their agency and efforts they had taken to address these challenges. We analyzed their responses and categorized them by topic.

We conducted our work from October 2011 through July 2012 in accordance with all sections of GAO's Quality Assurance Framework that were relevant to our objectives. The framework requires that we plan and perform the engagement to obtain sufficient and appropriate evidence to meet our stated objectives and to discuss any limitations in our work. We believe that the information obtained provides a reasonable basis for our findings and conclusions based on our audit objectives. Further details of our objectives, scope, and methodology are in appendix I.

---

[3]Results from a nongeneralizable sample cannot be used to make inferences about a population. To mitigate this limitation, our sample was designed to ensure we obtained highly-qualified users with a broad range of Agile experience across the private, public, and non-profit sectors.

Background

While federal IT investments can improve operational performance and increase public interaction with government, too often they have become risky, costly, and unproductive mistakes. Congress has expressed interest in monitoring and improving IT investments through hearings and other reviews over the past two decades. In response, we have testified and reported on lengthy federal IT projects that too frequently incur cost overruns and schedule slippages while contributing little to mission-related outcomes.[4] Similarly, in 2010, OMB expressed concern about expansive federal IT projects that have taken years and have failed at alarming rates. OMB also noted that many projects follow "grand designs" to deliver functionality in years, rather than breaking projects into more manageable chunks and delivering functionality every few quarters.

One approach to reducing the risks from broadly scoped, multiyear projects is the use of shorter software delivery times, a technique advocated by OMB in recent guidance documents. Specifically, OMB's June 2010 memo on IT financial system reforms and the December 2010 IT management reform plan[5] encourage modular development with usable functionality delivered in 90 to 120 days. In addition, the Federal Chief Information Officers (CIO) Council, chaired by OMB's Deputy Director for Management, encourages the sharing and adoption of efficient IT development practices, such as those in OMB's IT guidance. The Council is comprised of CIOs and Deputy CIOs of 28 agencies. It is

---

[4]See, for example, GAO, *Information Technology Reform: Progress Made: More Needs to Be Done to Complete Actions and Measure Results,* GAO-12-745T (Washington, D.C.: May 24, 2012); *FEMA: Action Needed to Improve Administration of the National Flood Insurance Program,* GAO-11-297 (Washington, D.C.: June 9, 2011); *Secure Border Initiative: DHS Needs to Reconsider Its Proposed Investment in Key Technology Program,* GAO-10-340 (Washington, D.C.: May 5, 2010); *Secure Border Initiative: DHS Needs to Address Testing and Performance Limitations That Place Key Technology Program at Risk,* GAO-10-158 (Washington, D.C.: Jan. 29, 2010); *Information Technology: Management and Oversight of Projects Totaling Billions of Dollars Need Attention,* GAO-09-624T (Washington, D.C.: Apr. 28, 2009); *Information Technology: Agriculture Needs to Strengthen Management Practices for Stabilizing and Modernizing Its Farm Program Delivery Systems,* GAO-08-657 (Washington, D.C.: May 16, 2008); *Information Technology: FBI Following a Number of Key Acquisition Practices on New Case Management System, but Improvements Still Needed,* GAO-07-912 (Washington, D.C.: July 30, 2007); *Information Technology: Foundational Steps Being Taken to Make Needed FBI Systems Modernization Management Improvements,* GAO-04-842 (Washington, D.C.: Sept.10, 2004); and GAO/HR-97-9.

[5]We recently reported on OMB's progress on these reforms in GAO, *Information Technology Reform: Progress Made; More Needs to Be Done to Complete Actions and Measure Results,* GAO-12-461 (Washington, D.C.: Apr. 26, 2012).

the principal interagency forum for improving agency practices related to the design, acquisition, development, modernization, use, sharing, and performance of federal information resources.

Agile software development supports the practice of shorter software delivery. Specifically, Agile calls for the delivery of software in small, short increments rather than in the typically long, sequential phases of a traditional waterfall approach. More a philosophy than a methodology, Agile emphasizes this early and continuous software delivery, as well as using collaborative teams, and measuring progress with working software. The Agile approach was first articulated in a 2001 document called the Agile Manifesto, which is still used today. The manifesto has four values: (1) individuals and interactions over processes and tools, (2) working software over comprehensive documentation, (3) customer collaboration over contract negotiation, and (4) responding to change over following a plan.[6] Appendix II provides additional information on the Agile Manifesto and its related principles.

Agile and Waterfall Approaches Differ

The Agile approach differs in several ways from traditional waterfall software development,[7] which produces a full software product at the end of a sequence of phases. For example, the two approaches differ in (1) the timing and scope of software development and delivery, (2) the timing and scope of project planning, (3) project status evaluation, and (4) collaboration.

- **Timing and scope of software development and delivery.** In an Agile project, working software is produced in iterations of typically one to eight weeks in duration, each of which provides a segment of functionality. To allow completion within the short time frame, each iteration is relatively small in scope. For example, an iteration could encompass a single function within a multistep process for documenting and reporting insurance claims, such as a data entry screen or a link to a database. Iterations combine into releases, with

---

[6]The Agile Manifesto was written by a group of methodologists called the Agile Alliance. For more information on the creation of the Agile Manifesto, go to http://agilemanifesto.org.

[7]For example, see the comparison of Agile and waterfall in Carnegie Mellon Software Engineering Institute, Mary Ann Lapham, et al., *Considerations for Using Agile in DOD Acquisition* (Pittsburgh, Pa: April 2010).

the number of iterations dependent on the scope of the multistep process. To meet the goal of delivering working software, teams perform each of the steps of traditional software development for each iteration. Specifically, for each iteration, the teams identify requirements, design, and develop software to meet those requirements, and test the resulting software to determine if it meets the stated requirements. In contrast, waterfall development proceeds in sequential phases of no consistent, fixed duration to produce a complete system, such as one that addresses a comprehensive set of steps to manage insurance claims. Such full system development efforts can take several years. Waterfall phases typically address a single step in the development cycle. For example, in one phase, customer requirements for the complete product are documented, reviewed, and handed to technical staff. One or more phases follow, in which the technical staff develop software to meet those requirements. In the final phase, the software is tested and reviewed for compliance with the identified requirements.

- **Timing and scope of project planning.** In Agile, initial planning regarding cost, scope, and timing is conducted at a high level. However, these initial plans are supplemented by more specific plans for each iteration and the overall plans can be revised to reflect experience from completed iterations. For example, desired project outcomes might initially be captured in a broad vision statement that provides the basis for developing specific outcomes for an iteration. Once an iteration has been completed, the overall plans can be revised to reflect the completed work and any knowledge gained during the iteration. For example, initial cost and schedule estimates can be revised to reflect the actual cost and timing of the completed work. In contrast, in traditional waterfall project management, this analysis is documented in detail at the beginning of the project for the entire scope of work. For example, significant effort may be devoted to documenting strategies, project plans, cost and schedule estimates, and requirements for a full system.

- **Project status evaluation.** In Agile, project status is primarily evaluated based on software demonstrations. For example, iterations typically end with a demonstration for customers and stakeholders of the working software produced during that iteration. The demonstration can reveal requirements that were not fully addressed during the iteration or the discovery of new requirements. These incomplete or newly-identified requirements are queued for possible inclusion in later iterations. In contrast, in traditional project management, progress is assessed based on a review of data and documents at predetermined milestones and checkpoints. Milestones and checkpoints can occur at the end of a phase, such as the end of requirements definition, or at scheduled intervals, such as monthly. The reviews typically include status reports on work done to date and a comparison of the project's actual cost and schedule to baseline projections. Federal IT evaluation guidance, such as our IT Investment Management guidance[8] and OMB IT reporting requirements[9] specify evaluations at key milestones, and annually, which more closely align with traditional development methods. For example, for major projects, OMB requires a monthly comparison of actual and planned cost and schedule and risk status and annual performance measures using, for example, earned value management (EVM).[10]

- **Collaboration.** Agile development emphasizes collaboration more than traditional approaches do. For example, to coordinate the many disciplines of an iteration, such as design and testing, customers work frequently and closely with technical staff. Furthermore, teams are often self-directed, meaning tasks and due dates are done within the team and coordinated with project sponsors and stakeholders as needed to complete the tasks. In contrast, with traditional project management, customer and technical staff typically work separately, and project tasks are prescribed and monitored by a project manager, who reports to entities such as a program management office.

See figure 1 for a depiction of Agile development compared to waterfall development.

---

[8]GAO, *Information Technology Investment Management: A Framework for Assessing and Improving Process Maturity,* GAO-04-394G (Washington, D.C.: March 2004).

[9]For certain IT investments, OMB requires an annual report called the exhibit 300 and monthly status on a website called the IT Dashboard (http://www.itdashboard.gov/).

[10]EVM is a tool for measuring a project's progress by comparing the value of work accomplished with the amount of work expected to be completed, and is based on variances from cost and schedule baselines.

Figure 1: Comparison of Agile and Waterfall Development

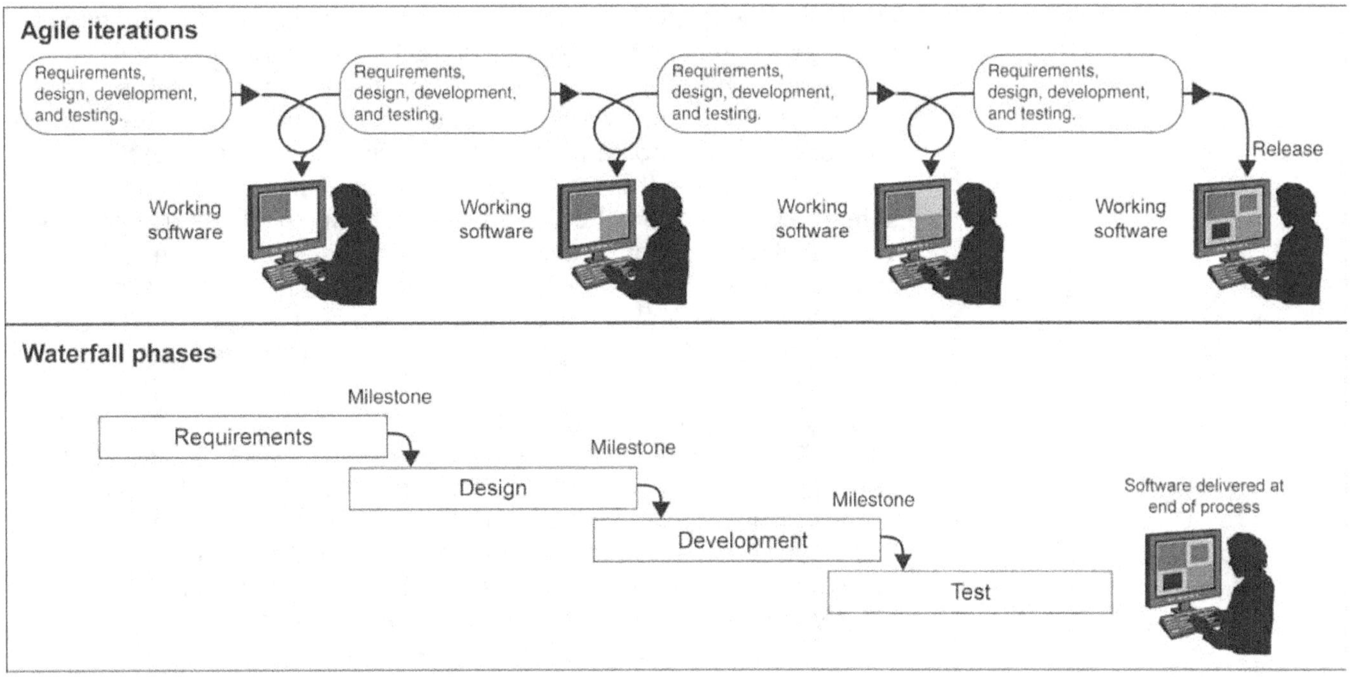

Source: GAO.

Agile Frameworks

There are numerous frameworks available to Agile practitioners. One framework, called eXtreme Programming (XP), includes development techniques.[11] Another framework, called Scrum, defines management processes and roles. The Scrum framework is widely used in the public and private sector, and its terminology is often used in Agile discussions. For example, Scrum iterations are called sprints, which are bundled into releases. Sprint teams collaborate with minimal management direction, often co-located in work rooms. They meet daily and post their task status visibly, such as on wall charts.

Other concepts commonly used by sprint teams are user stories, story points, and backlog. User stories convey the customers' requirements. A

---

[11]For example, XP includes technical practices such as test-driven development, in which the test of software code to meet a requirement is written before writing the operational code.

user story typically follows the construct of "As a <type of user> I want <some goal> so that <some reason>." For example, "As a claims processor, I want to check a claim payment status so that I can promptly reply to a customer's request for payment status." Each user story is assigned a level of effort, called story points, which are a relative unit of measure used to communicate complexity and progress between the business and development sides of the project. To ensure that the product is usable at the end of every iteration, teams adhere to an agreed-upon definition of done. This includes stakeholders defining how completed work conforms to an organization's standards, conventions, and guidelines. The backlog is a list of user stories to be addressed by working software. If new requirements or defects are discovered, these can be stored in the backlog to be addressed in future iterations.

Progress in automating user stories is tracked daily using metrics and tools. An example of a metric is velocity. Velocity tracks the rate of work using the number of story points completed or expected to be completed in an iteration. For example, if a team completed 100 story points during a four-week iteration, the velocity for the team would be 100 story points every four weeks. An example of a tool is a burn-down chart, which tracks progress and the amount of work remaining for an iteration or for a release, which is made up of multiple iterations.

Agile in the Private and Federal Sectors

Agile use is reported in the private sector for small to medium sized projects and is starting to be used for larger projects as well. Also, widely accepted industry guidance on software development has recently been revised to include more Agile approaches. Specifically, the Software Engineering Institute's Capability Maturity Model® Integration[12] updated some process areas to help those using Agile to interpret its practices.

Furthermore, the federal government has begun to use Agile. For example, we have reported on several federal software development efforts that have used Agile techniques. Specifically, in December 2010

---

[12]The Software Engineering Institute is a nationally recognized, federally funded research and development center established at Carnegie Mellon University to address software engineering practices. The institute has developed process maturity models for software development, including CMMI® for Development, Version 1.3, *Improving Processes for Developing Better Products and Services*, (Pittsburgh, Pa: November 2010).

we reported[13] that the Department of Veterans Affairs was using Agile to develop software to support a new benefit for veterans. We also reported[14] that the Department of Defense was developing the Global Combat Support System-Joint system using Agile. In addition, the department sponsored studies that examined the possibility of more widespread use of Agile in its development projects.[15]

Effective Practices for Applying Agile

We identified 32 practices and approaches[16] as effective for applying Agile to software development projects, based on an analysis of practices identified by experienced Agile users. Our analysis also found that the identified practices generally align with five key project management activities outlined in widely-accepted software development guidance: strategic planning, organizational commitment and collaboration, preparation, execution, and evaluation.

Strategic Planning

Strategic planning describes an organization's overall plans in an Agile environment. Six practices align with strategic planning. They are:

- **Strive to be more Agile, rather than simply following Agile methods and steps.** This approach encourages adoption of the philosophy, or mindset, rather than specific steps. This is also referred to as being Agile, or having agility versus using it.

- **Allow for a gradual migration to Agile appropriate to your readiness.** Migration steps might include combining Agile and

---

[13]GAO, *Information Technology: Veterans Affairs Can Further Improve Its Development Process for Its New Education Benefits System,* GAO-11-115 (Washington, D.C.: Dec. 1, 2010).

[14]GAO-12-7.

[15]Carnegie Mellon Software Engineering Institute, Mary Ann Lapham, et al., *Considerations for Using Agile in DOD Acquisition* (Pittsburgh, Pa: April 2010); and *Agile Methods: Selected DOD Management and Acquisition Concerns* (Pittsburgh, Pa: October 2011).

[16]Although we asked the experienced users to identify effective practices, several of the items they identified can be considered more of an approach, or way to think about proceeding, than practices that describe how something should be done. This aligns with the concept of Agile being as much a philosophy as a set of steps to be followed.

existing methods, conducting pilots, and preparing technical infrastructure.

- **Observe and communicate with other organizations implementing Agile.** For example, those starting to use Agile can consult with others who have more experience, including academic, private sector, and federal practitioners.

- **Follow organizational change disciplines, such as establishing a sense of urgency and developing a change vision.** A clear vision of change helps staff understand what the organization is trying to achieve. Another organizational change discipline is communication strategies.

- **Be prepared for difficulties, regression, and negative attitudes.** This approach reinforces that Agile is not painless and users may backslide to entrenched software methods.

- **Start with Agile guidance and an Agile adoption strategy.** This practice advocates having these elements in place at the start, even if they must be copied from external sources.

Organizational Commitment and Collaboration

Organizational commitment describes the management actions that are necessary to ensure that a process is established and will endure. Collaboration in Agile typically refers to the close and frequent interaction of teams. Four practices align with organizational commitment and collaboration:

- **Ensure all components involved in Agile projects are committed to the organization's Agile approach.** This practice encourages organizations to ensure that everyone contributing to a project understands and commits to the organization's approach. This includes those working directly on the project and those with less direct involvement, such as those providing oversight.

- **Identify an Agile champion within senior management.** This practice calls for someone with formal authority within the organization to advocate the approach and resolve impediments at this level.

- **Ensure all teams include coaches or staff with Agile experience.** This practice stresses the importance of including on each team those with direct experience in applying Agile. While training is helpful, hands on experience helps the team members learn and adjust.

- **Empower small, cross-functional teams.** Empowered teams of 7 to 18 people decide what to deliver and how to produce it. The teams should not over-rely on one member's skills.

Preparation

Taking certain preparatory steps prior to the start of an iteration can facilitate a rapid development pace. The following eight practices generally align with the preparation of people and processes.

- **Train the entire organization in your Agile approach and mindset, and train Agile practitioners in your Agile methods.** For example, managers must understand the approach so that they know how it will affect them and teams need to know the specific steps of an iteration to conduct it properly.

- **Ensure that subject matter experts and business team members have the required knowledge.** This practice stresses that staff involved in fast-paced iterations must truly be experts in the processes being automated in that iteration in order to reduce delays. For example, a team member representing financial customers must be fully familiar with the needs of those customers.

- **Enhance migration to Agile concepts using Agile terms and examples.** For example, use terms like user stories instead of requirements, and Agile Center of Excellence instead of Project Management Office. Provide examples, such as one illustrating the small scope of a user story to teams writing these stories.

- **Create a physical environment conducive to collaboration.** A common practice is to co-locate the team in a single room where they can continually interact. Other ways to enhance collaboration are to reorganize office space and use tools to connect remote staff.

- **Identify measurable outcomes, not outputs, of what you want to achieve using Agile.** An example of this practice is creating a vision statement of project outcomes (such as a decrease in processing time by a specific percent in a set time), rather than outputs (such as the amount of code produced).

- **Negotiate to adjust oversight requirements to a more Agile approach.** This practice notes that teams may be able to adjust oversight requirements by using frequent, tangible demonstrations to gain the trust of reviewers and investors, potentially reducing the need for more formal oversight documents.

- **Ensure that the definition of how a story will be determined to be done is comprehensive and objective.** Comprehensiveness includes defining what constitutes a finished product (i.e., packaged, documented, tested, and independently verified). Objective means measurable or verifiable versus subjective judgment.

- **Make contracts flexible to accommodate your Agile approach.** Contracts requiring waterfall-based artifacts and milestone reviews may not support the frequent changes and product demonstrations in iterations, and may inhibit adoption.

Execution

Execution entails the concrete steps necessary to conduct the iteration following the designated approach. The seven identified practices that align with execution are:

- **Use the same duration for each iteration.** An example would be establishing that iterations will be four weeks each within a release to establish a uniform pace.

- **Combine Agile frameworks such as Scrum and XP if appropriate.** Disciplines from different frameworks can be combined. For example, use project management disciplines from Scrum and technical practices from XP.

- **Enhance early customer involvement and design using test-driven development.** Test-driven development refers to writing software code to pass a test. This practice maintains that involving customers in these tests helps to engage them in the software development process.

- **Include requirements related to security and progress monitoring in your queue of unfinished work (backlog).** Including activities such as security reviews and status briefings in the backlog ensures their time and cost are reflected and that they are addressed concurrent with, and not after, iteration delivery.

- **Capture iteration defects in a tool such as a backlog.** This practice calls for queuing issues so that they are resolved in later iterations. For example, lists of unmet requirements generated at end-of-iteration demonstrations should be queued in the backlog for correction in a future iteration.

- **Expedite delivery using automated tools.** For example, tools can track software modifications, and compliant development sites or "sandboxes" help customers conceptualize the software in an environment that meets architectural and security standards.

- **Test early and often throughout the life cycle.** The theme of this practice is that testing during software code delivery instead of after delivery reduces risk and remediation costs.

Evaluation

Evaluations can occur at the project and organizational level. For example, at the project level, the iteration is reviewed at its completion in a retrospective. At the organizational level, processes are reviewed for opportunities to improve the approach. The following seven practices align with evaluation:

- **Obtain stakeholder/customer feedback frequently and closely.** For example, feedback is obtained during the iteration and at its completion at an iteration retrospective. This practice was linked to reducing risk, improving customer commitment, and improving technical staff motivation.

- **Continuously improve Agile adoption at both the project level and organization level.** This practice invokes the discipline of continuous improvement, meaning always looking for ways to improve. For example, improvements can be made by adding automated test and version control tools, and enhancing team rooms. These issues can be tracked in project and organizational-level backlogs.

- **Seek to identify and address impediments at the organization and project levels.** This practice encourages organizations to be frank about identifying impediments so that they can be addressed.

- **Determine project value based on customer perception and return on investment.** This practice recognizes that tracking progress only against cost or schedule criteria set before the project began could lead to inaccurate measurement of progress if, for example, major changes in scope occur. Instead, Agile encourages customer feedback as one measure of progress. Comparing solution value to the cost of the solution is also a gauge of success.

- **Gain trust by demonstrating value at the end of each iteration.** This practice includes demonstrating key requirements in early iterations, and showing customers that requirements in the backlog are delivered and not forgotten.

- **Track progress using tools and metrics.** Progress can be tracked using tools and metrics such as burn-down charts and velocity, which can be automated, and by success indicators such as "customer delight," and reduced staff stress and overtime.

- **Track progress daily and visibly.** This practice stresses that status is checked daily and publicly. For example, a progress chart is posted openly in the team's workspace, with timely revisions to reflect ongoing feedback.

Federal Use of Effective Practices

Officials who have used Agile on federal projects at five agencies generally agreed that the practices identified by the experienced users are effective in a federal setting. Specifically, each practice was used and found effective by officials from at least one agency. Ten of the 32 practices were used and found effective by officials at all five agencies (see table 1).

Table 1: Practices Used and Found Effective by Five Agencies

Practice
1. Start with Agile guidance and an Agile adoption strategy.
2. Enhance migration to Agile concepts using Agile terms and examples.
3. Continuously improve Agile adoption at both project and organization levels.
4. Seek to identify and address impediments at the organization and project levels.
5. Obtain stakeholder/customer feedback frequently and closely.
6. Empower small, cross-functional teams.
7. Include requirements related to security and progress monitoring in your queue of unfinished work (backlog).
8. Gain trust by demonstrating value at the end of each iteration.
9. Track progress using tools and metrics.
10. Track progress daily and visibly.

Source: GAO.

Also, in most cases, a practice was still believed to be effective even if it was not used. For example, officials explained that they did not use a practice they indicated was effective because it was not appropriate for their project or that they used an alternate practice.

Although the identified practices were generally described as effective, officials from three agencies each reported one practice they had used but found to be not effective. According to the agency officials, two practices were identified as ineffective because they were difficult to implement. These practices were: (1) ensuring commitment from components and (2) negotiating oversight requirements. The third practice, striving to be Agile rather than simply following Agile methods, was described by an agency official as not effective because he believed that strict adherence was necessary for a successful project.

Federal Challenges in Applying Agile

We identified 14 challenges with adapting to and applying Agile in the federal environment based on an analysis of experiences collected from five federal agencies that had applied Agile to a development effort. These challenges relate to significant differences in not only how software is developed but also how projects are managed in an Agile development environment versus a waterfall development environment. We aligned the challenges with four of the project management activities used to organize effective practices: (1) ensuring organizational commitment and collaboration, (2) preparing for Agile, (3) executing development in an Agile environment, and (4) evaluating the product and project. In addition to identifying challenges, federal officials described efforts underway at their agencies to address these challenges.

Organizational Commitment and Collaboration

As described in the effective practices, Agile projects require the ongoing collaboration and commitment of a wide array of stakeholders, including business owners, developers, and security specialists. One way Agile promotes commitment and collaboration is by having teams work closely together, in one location, with constant team communication. Officials at the selected agencies identified challenges in achieving and maintaining such commitment and collaboration from their stakeholders as follows.

- **Teams had difficulty collaborating closely:** Officials from three agencies reported that teams were challenged in collaborating because staff were used to working independently. For example, one official reported that staff were challenged when asked to relocate to a team room because the technical staff preferred to work alone. The official added that some staff viewed open communication, such as posting project status on team room wall charts, as intrusive. A second official said that technical staff did not like constantly showing their work to customers. The third official said that customers initially did not want to see such development, preferring to wait for a polished product.

- **Teams had difficulty transitioning to self-directed work:** Officials at two agencies reported that staff had challenges in transitioning to self-directed teams. In Agile, teams made up of customers and technical staff are encouraged to create and manage their tasks without project manager direction and to elevate issues to stakeholders who have the authority to resolve them. Cross functionality is also encouraged to allow teams to share tasks. One official reported that teams used to direction from a project manager were challenged in taking responsibility for their work and in elevating issues they could not resolve within the team to senior officials. A second official noted that it was a challenge to create cross-functional teams because federal staff tend to be specialists in one functional area. An example of this would be where a team could include someone to represent system users, but that person may not be familiar with the needs of all users. Specifically, a team developing an insurance system might include someone with a background in claims processing. However, that person may not be experienced with payment procedures.

- **Staff had difficulty committing to more timely and frequent input:** While Agile advocates frequent input and feedback from all stakeholders, four agency officials noted challenges to commit to meeting such input expectations. One agency official noted that individuals were challenged to commit to keeping work products, such as schedules, updated to reflect the status of every iteration because they were not used to this rapid pace. A second official stated that teams initially had difficulty maintaining the pace of an iteration because they were used to stopping their work to address issues rather than making a decision and moving on. A third official said that it was challenging incorporating security requirements at the rapid pace of the sprint. A fourth official said customer availability was a challenge because customers initially did not understand the amount and pace of the time commitment for Agile and needed to develop a mindset to attend meetings as well as frequently review deliverables.

- **Agencies had trouble committing staff:** Three agency officials reported being challenged assigning and maintaining staff commitments to projects. The frequent input expected of staff involved in projects requires a more significant time commitment than that required for waterfall development projects that allow more sporadic participation. For example, two officials said their agencies were challenged dedicating staff with multiple, concurrent duties to teams because staff could not be spared from their other duties while participating in the Agile teams. The third official said stakeholder commitment is challenging to maintain when stakeholders rotate frequently and new staff need to learn the roles and responsibilities of those being replaced.

Preparation

When an organization following waterfall software development migrates to Agile, new tools and technical environments may be required to support that approach, as well as updates to guidance and procurement strategies. Officials described challenges in preparing for Agile as follows.

- **Timely adoption of new tools was difficult:** As identified in the effective practices, automated tools may be used to support project planning and reporting. One official noted that implementing Agile tools that aid in planning and reporting progress was initially a challenge because there was a delay in buying, installing, and learning to use these tools.

- **Technical environments were difficult to establish and maintain:** Two agency officials noted that establishing and maintaining technical environments posed challenges because Agile calls for development, test, and operational activities to be performed concurrently. According to one agency's officials, preparing and maintaining synchronized hardware and software environments for these three activities in time to support the releases was expensive to support and logistically challenging. Furthermore, one of these officials noted that his agency experienced a challenge running multiple concurrent iterations because this required more complex coordination of staff and resources.

- **Agile guidance was not clear:** Officials from three agencies identified a challenge related to the lack of clear guidance for Agile software development, particularly when agency software development guidance reflected a waterfall approach. For example, one official said that it was challenging to develop policy and procedure guidance for iterative projects because they were new, and the agency strategy aligned with the waterfall approach. As a result, it was difficult to ensure that iterative projects could follow a standard

GAO-12-681 Agile Effective Practices and Federal Challenges

approach. A second official reported that deviating from waterfall-based procedural guidance to follow Agile methods made people nervous. For example, staff were nervous following team versus project manager directed tasks because this approach was not in their IT guidance. A third official said that their guidance mixed iterative and waterfall life cycle approaches, which staff found confusing.

- **Procurement practices may not support Agile projects:** Agile projects call for flexibility adding the staff and resources needed to meet each iteration, and to adapt to changes from one iteration to the next. One official stated that working with federal procurement practices presents a challenge where they do not support the flexibility required. For example, he said that federal contracts that require onerous, waterfall-based artifacts to constantly evaluate contractor performance are not needed in an Agile approach when the contractor is part of the team whose performance is based on the delivery of an iteration. Furthermore, the official said that they are challenged changing contractor staff in time to meet iteration time frames and that accommodating task changes from one iteration to the next is challenging because contracting officers require cumbersome traditional structured tasks and performance checks.

Execution

As described in the effective practices, Agile projects develop software iteratively, incorporating requirements and product development within an iteration. Such requirements may include compliance with agency legal and policy requirements. Officials reported challenges executing steps related to iterative development and compliance reviews as follows.

- **Customers did not trust iterative solutions:** Agile software products are presented to customers incrementally, for approval at the end of each iteration, instead of presenting complete products for approval at waterfall milestones. Officials at two agencies reported a challenge related to customer mistrust of iterative solutions. Specifically, one agency official said customers expecting a total solution feared that the initial demonstrations of functionality provided in the current iteration would be considered good enough, and they would not receive further software deliveries implementing the remainder of their requirements. At another agency, an official said this fear contributed to customers finding it difficult to define done. Specifically, customers were challenged in defining when each requirement would be considered done because they were afraid that this would be viewed as meaning all related functions were being met, and that unmet requirements would be dropped and never implemented.

- **Teams had difficulty managing iterative requirements:** Teams provide input on prioritizing requirements, and deciding what to do with new requirements discovered during iterations. Two agencies' officials reported challenges managing requirements. Specifically, one official reported that customers were initially challenged to validate and prioritize which requirements would be assigned to a release. Using the waterfall development model, they were used to identifying all requirements up front and not revisiting them as they were developed. The second official said they were challenged to accommodate new requirements within the fixed schedule for a product release.

- **Compliance reviews were difficult to execute within an iteration time frame:** Iterations may incorporate compliance reviews to ensure, for example, that agency legal and policy requirements are being met within the iteration. One agency official reported a challenge obtaining compliance reviews within the short, fixed time frame of an iteration because reviewers followed a slower waterfall schedule. Specifically, the official said that compliance reviewers queued requests as they arose and that the reviews could take months to perform. This caused delays for iterations that needed such reviews within the few weeks of the iteration.

Evaluation

Agile advocates evaluation of working software over the documentation and milestone reporting typical in traditional project management. Officials described challenges in evaluating projects related to the lack of alignment between Agile and traditional evaluation practices. Specifically, officials explained that:

- **Federal reporting practices do not align with Agile:** Two agency officials noted that several federal reporting practices do not align with Agile, creating challenges. For example, one official said federal oversight bodies want status reports at waterfall-based milestones rather than timely statements regarding the current state of the project. The second official said OMB's IT investment business case (known as the exhibit 300) and IT Dashboard, a publicly available website that displays detailed information on federal agencies' major IT investments,[17] are waterfall-based. For example, the IT Dashboard calls for monthly statistics instead of demonstrations of working software. He also noted that it is frustrating when dashboard statistics are flagged in red to note deviations, even when the deviation is positive, such as being ahead of schedule and under cost.

- **Traditional artifact reviews do not align with Agile:** Traditional oversight requires detailed artifacts in the beginning of a project, such as cost estimates and strategic plans, while Agile advocates incremental analysis. One agency official noted that requiring these artifacts so early was challenging because it was more worthwhile to start with a high-level cost estimate and vision to be updated as the solution was refined through iterations, rather than spending time estimating costs and strategies that may change.

- **Traditional status tracking does not align with Agile:** Officials from three agencies noted that project status tracking in Agile does not align with traditional status tracking methods, creating challenges. For example, one official said that tracking the level of effort using story points instead of the traditional estimating technique based on hours was a challenge because team members were not used to that estimation method, although eventually this method was embraced. Two other agency officials said EVM was challenging to apply in an Agile environment. Specifically, one official said that the required use of EVM was challenging because there was no guidance on how to adapt it to iterations. The second official found EVM challenging because the agency was required to use it to track changes in cost, schedule, and product scope through monthly reports, and changes were viewed as control problems rather than as revisions to be expected during an iteration. For example, the project's scope was prioritized within every iteration based on the cost and schedule limits of the iteration and release. He also noted that risk tracking in Agile does not align with traditional risk tracking methods because issues are addressed within an iteration rather than queued, such as in a traditional monthly risk log.

---

[17]The IT Dashboard includes assessments of actual performance against cost and schedule targets (referred to as ratings) for approximately 800 major federal IT investments. The IT Dashboard website is located at http://www.itdashboard.gov/.

In addition to identifying challenges, federal officials described their efforts to address these challenges. For example, officials said they clarify policies to address the challenge of Agile guidance lacking clarity. To mitigate the challenge related to customers not trusting iterative solutions, an official said they call the iteration review a mini-critical design review. This helps customers understand that they must declare the iteration complete or not, known as committing to done. Another official said one way that they addressed the challenge related to teams having difficulty managing iterative requirements was to add an empty iteration to the end of the release schedule to accommodate requirements discovered during the iterations.

In addition to the efforts at individual agencies to mitigate Agile challenges, the Federal CIO Council has begun an effort on a related topic. According to an official working with the Council, it is currently drafting a document on modular development. Consistent with OMB's IT reform efforts, the document is expected to provide guidance for agencies seeking to use more modular development approaches, such as Agile. However, according to the official, the draft does not specifically address Agile effective practices. Also, in June 2012 OMB released contracting guidance to support modular development.[18] This guidance includes factors for contracting officers to consider for modular development efforts regarding for example, statements of work, pricing arrangements, and small business opportunities.

Conclusions

As Agile methods begin to be more broadly used in federal development projects, agencies in the initial stages of adopting Agile can benefit from the knowledge of those with more experience. The ongoing effort by the Federal CIO Council to develop guidance on modular development provides an excellent opportunity to share these experiences. The effective practices and approaches identified in this report, as well as input from others with broad Agile experience, can inform this effort.

---

[18]OMB, *Contracting Guidance to Support Modular Development* (Washington, D.C.: June 2012).

Recommendation for Executive Action

To ensure that the experiences of those who have used Agile development are shared broadly, we recommend that the Federal CIO Council, working with its chair, the Office of Management and Budget's Deputy Director for Management, include practices such as those discussed in this report in the Council's ongoing effort to promote modular development in the federal government.

Agency Comments and Our Evaluation

We provided a draft of our report to OMB and to the five federal agencies included in our review. In oral comments on the draft, OMB's E-government program manager said that the draft recommendation was better addressed to the Federal CIO Council than to the OMB official who is the chair of the Council. Accordingly, we revised the recommendation to address it to the Council, working with its chair, the OMB Deputy Director for Management. Two of the five agencies provided written comments on the draft, which are reprinted in appendix V and VI. Specifically, the Department of Veterans Affairs Chief of Staff stated that the department generally agreed with the draft's findings, and the Acting Secretary of the Department of Commerce stated that the Patent and Trademark Office concurred with our assessment. Two other agencies, the Internal Revenue Service and the Department of Defense, provided technical comments via e-mail, which we incorporated as appropriate. In an e-mail, a manager in the National Aeronautics and Space Administration (NASA) center included in our review said that NASA had no comments.

As agreed with your offices, we will send copies of this report to interested congressional committees; the Secretaries of Defense, Commerce, and Veterans Affairs; the Administrator of NASA and the Commissioner of Internal Revenue; the Director of the Office of Management and Budget; and other interested parties. In addition, the report will be available at no charge on our website at http://www.gao.gov.

If you or your staff have any questions on the matters discussed in this report, please contact David A. Powner at (202) 512-9286 or Dr. Nabajyoti Barkakati at (202) 512-4499 or by e-mail at pownerd@gao.gov or barkakatin@gao.gov. Contact points for our Offices of Congressional Relations and Public Affairs may be found on the last page of this report. GAO staff who made major contributions to this report are listed in appendix VII.

David A. Powner
Director
Information Technology
Management Issues

Dr. Nabajyoti Barkakati
Director
Center for Technology and Engineering

Appendix I: Objectives, Scope, and Methodology

Our objectives were to identify (1) effective practices in applying Agile for software development solutions and (2) federal challenges in implementing Agile development techniques.

To identify effective practices, we interviewed a nongeneralizable sample of nine experienced users and a tenth experienced user helped us pre-test our data collection process.[1] To identify these users, we researched publications, attended forums, and obtained recommendations from federal and private officials knowledgeable about Agile. We selected individuals with Agile software development experience with public, private sector, and non-profit organizations. Using a structured interview, we asked them to identify effective practices when applying Agile methods to software development projects. We then compiled the reported practices and aligned and combined some with a broader practice. For example, practices related to preparation, such as mock and pilot iterations, were aligned and then combined into the final practice, "Allow for a gradual migration to Agile appropriate to your readiness." If a practice did not align with other or broader practices, it was listed individually.

We then sent the resulting list of practices in a questionnaire to our experienced users. This list was not organized into categories to ensure that each practice would be viewed individually. We asked our users to rate each practice as either (1) highly effective, (2) moderately effective, (3) somewhat effective, or (4) not applicable/do not know. We compiled the ratings and included in our list the practices that received at least six ratings of highly effective or moderately effective from the 8 experienced users who provided the requested ratings.[2] This resulted in 32 practices, which we aligned to key project management activities in Software Engineering Institute guidance: strategic planning, organizational commitment and collaboration, preparation, execution, and evaluation. This alignment was based on our best judgment.

---

[1]Results from nongeneralizable samples cannot be used to make inferences about a population. To mitigate this limitation, our sample was designed to ensure we obtained highly-qualified users with a broad range of Agile experience across the private, public, and non-profit sectors.

[2]The ninth experienced user was asked for input on the list of practices with the others, but did not respond in time to meet our reporting deadline.

To identify federal challenges, we interviewed officials responsible for five
federal software development projects that reported using Agile practices.
To identify the projects, we researched our previous work, federal
websites, and publications, and attended federal forums. We selected a
nongeneralizable sample of projects designed to reflect a range of
agencies, system descriptions, and cost (see app. IV for details about the
projects and the responsible officials). We then asked officials from each
project to identify federal challenges in implementing an Agile approach
using a structured interview. We summarized the challenges and
categorized them as aligning with either organizational commitment and
collaboration, preparation, execution, or evaluation. Separately, we sent
the federal officials a questionnaire listing the effective practices we
compiled based on input from our experienced users. The questionnaire
asked whether these practices were used and found effective. Although
our results are not generalizable to the population of software
development projects reporting the use of Agile practices, they provided
valuable insight into both the effective use and challenges in applying
Agile in the federal sector.

We conducted our work from October 2011 through July 2012 in
accordance with all sections of GAO's Quality Assurance Framework that
are relevant to our objectives. The framework requires that we plan and
perform the engagement to obtain sufficient and appropriate evidence to
meet our stated objectives and to discuss any limitations in our work. We
believe that the information obtained provides a reasonable basis for our
findings and conclusions based on our audit objectives.

Appendix II: The Agile Manifesto and Principles

Agile development encompasses concepts that were previously used in software development. These concepts were documented as Agile themes and principles by 17 practitioners, who called themselves the Agile Alliance. In February 2001 the Alliance released "The Agile Manifesto,"[1] in which they declared: "We are uncovering better ways of developing software by doing it and helping others do it. Through this work we have come to value:

- individuals and interactions over processes and tools

- working software over comprehensive documentation

- customer collaboration over contract negotiation

- responding to change over following a plan."

The Alliance added that while they recognized the value in the second part of each statement (i.e., "processes and tools"), they saw more value in the first part ("individuals and interactions"). The Alliance further delineated their vision with twelve principles.

The 12 Agile Principles behind the Manifesto

- Our highest priority is to satisfy the customer through early and continuous delivery of valuable software.

- Welcome changing requirements, even late in development. Agile processes harness change for the customer's competitive advantage.

- Deliver working software frequently, from a couple of weeks to a couple of months, with a preference to the shorter timescale.

- Business people and developers must work together daily throughout the project.

- Build projects around motivated individuals. Give them the environment and support they need, and trust them to get the job done.

---

[1] http://agilemanifesto.org.

- The most efficient and effective method of conveying information to and within a development team is face-to-face conversation.

- Working software is the primary measure of progress.

- Agile processes promote sustainable development. The sponsors, developers, and users should be able to maintain a constant pace indefinitely.

- Continuous attention to technical excellence and good design enhances agility.

- Simplicity—the art of maximizing the amount of work not done—is essential.

- The best architectures, requirements, and designs emerge from self-organizing teams.

- At regular intervals, the team reflects on how to become more effective, then tunes and adjusts its behavior accordingly.

Appendix III: Experienced Users

We interviewed the following experienced users to identify effective Agile practices. With one exception, they also contributed to the validation of our list of effective practices.

- Scott W. Ambler—Chief Methodologist for IT, IBM Rational

- Sanjiv Augustine—President, Lithespeed Consulting

- Gregor Bailar—Consultant

- Dr. Alan W. Brown—IBM Distinguished Engineer, Rational CTO for Europe, IBM Software Group

- Neil Chaudhuri—President, Vidya, L.L.C; Senior Software Engineer, Potomac Fusion

- Jerome Frese—Senior Enterprise Life Cycle Coach, Internal Revenue Service

- Dr. Steven J. Hutchison—Senior Executive, Office of the Secretary of Defense; Acquisition, Technology, and Logistics

- Mary Ann Lapham—Senior Member Technical Staff, Software Engineering Institute, Carnegie Mellon University

- Greg Pfister—Vice President Software Engineering, Agilex Technologies

- Bob Schatz—Senior Consultant and Advisor, Agile Infusion LLC

Appendix IV: Federal Project Profiles

The five federal software development projects that reported challenges in applying Agile practices are profiled as follows.

Global Combat Support System-Joint Increment 7

Table 2: Profile of Global Combat Support System-J Increment 7

Agency	Department of Defense, Defense Information Systems Agency
System description	Supports logistics operations such as mission supplies for military personnel.
Agile approach	Scrum
Estimated cost	$192.3 million over a 5-year period
Officials interviewed included	Project and deputy project managers

Source: Agency data.

National Aeronautics and Space Administration Enterprise Applications Competency Center Materials Management Initiative

Table 3: Profile of National Aeronautics and Space Administration Enterprise Applications Competency Center Materials Management Initiative

Agency	National Aeronautics and Space Administration
System description	Supports receipt, warehousing, inventory, and issuance of operating materials and supplies.
Agile approach	Scrum
Estimated cost	$6.6 million
Officials interviewed included	Civilian project manager and manager in the National Aeronautics and Space Administration Enterprise Application Competency Center

Source: Agency data.

Patents End-to-End

Table 4: Profile of Patents End-to-End

Agency	Department of Commerce, Patent and Trademark Office
System description	Supports end-to-end electronic patent processing.
Agile approach	Scrum
Estimated cost	$150 million over 5 years
Officials interviewed included	Chief information officer, deputy chief information officer, patents portfolio manager, and other project managers

Source: Agency data.

Occupational Health Record-keeping System

Table 5: Profile of Occupational Health Record-keeping System

Agency	Department of Veterans Affairs, Veterans Health Administration
System description	Supports private employee health records.
Agile approach	Scrum
Estimated cost	$20 million for development and operation
Officials interviewed included	Current and previous IT project managers

Source: Agency data.

Affordable Care Act Branded Prescription Drugs

Table 6: Profile of Affordable Care Act Branded Prescription Drugs

Agency	Internal Revenue Service
System description	Supports pharmaceutical fee and payment tracking.
Agile approach	Iterative with some Agile practices
Estimated cost	$40 to $44M over 10 years
Officials interviewed included	Associate chief information officer and program manager

Source: Agency data.

Appendix V: Comments from the Department of Veterans Affairs

DEPARTMENT OF VETERANS AFFAIRS
Washington DC 20420

July 10, 2012

Mr. David Powner
Director, Information Technology
   Management Issues
U.S. Government Accountability Office
441 G Street, NW
Washington, DC 20548

Dear Mr. Powner:

    The Department of Veterans Affairs (VA) has reviewed the Government Accountability Office's (GAO) draft report, *"SOFTWARE DEVELOPMENT: Effective Practices and Federal Challenges in Applying Agile Methods"* (GAO-12-681). VA generally agrees with GAO's findings.

    The enclosure contains general comments related to the draft report. VA appreciates the opportunity to comment on your draft report.

               Sincerely,

               John R. Gingrich
               Chief of Staff

Enclosure

Enclosure

Department of Veterans Affairs (VA) Comments to
Government Accountability Office (GAO) Draft Report
*"SOFTWARE DEVELOPMENT: Effective Practices and Federal Challenges
in Applying Agile Methods"*
(GAO-12-681)

General Comment:

Agile development is important to VA because it encourages continuous input from our
customers and requires quality assurance throughout the entire development effort,
ensuring high quality deliverables. In Agile projects, all the development priorities are
set by the customer, which ensures that the work is performed in the order of
importance. To increase the likelihood of success, large projects are broken down into
small but valuable increments, each of which is a candidate for release. This is
consistent with our Project Management Accountability System (PMAS) delivery
requirements. Whereas PMAS addresses the planning and management aspects of
short, incremental delivery, the Agile development methodology provides the technical
management guidance of how to quickly turn project requirements into working software
and in collaboration with the customer.

Agile software development methodologies are an effective means of improving the
predictability, quality, and transparency of VA software products and their development.
At the core of Agile is the iterative work process. Business problems are broken down
into small increments of delivery that are tangible products that can be reviewed and
verified regularly by business stakeholders. By constantly incorporating feedback, the
software that is essential to solving the business problem is created in partnership with
stakeholders and any miscommunications, revisions, or changes in business needs can
be accommodated quickly and efficiently. The quality of software is kept high
throughout the development process.

1

Appendix VI: Comments from the Department of Commerce

UNITED STATES DEPARTMENT OF COMMERCE
The Secretary of Commerce
Washington, D.C. 20230

July 11, 2012

Mr. David A. Powner
Director, Information Technology Management Issues
U.S. Government Accountability Office
441 G Street, NW
Washington, DC 20548

Dear Mr. Powner:

The U.S. Department of Commerce is pleased to provide a response to the U.S.
Government Accountability Office's (GAO) draft report entitled "Software Development:
Effective Practices and Federal Challenges in Applying Agile Methods" (GAO-12-681).
The GAO conducted an evaluation of effective practices and federal challenges in applying
Agile information technology development methods.

The United States Patent and Trademark Office (USPTO) participated in the interviews that
led to the findings of the report and concurs with the GAO assessment of the best practices and
challenges. The USPTO will continue to refine their processes to align with effective practices
and will continue to address the challenges identified in the effective use of Agile methods in the
Federal Government.

Sincerely,

Rebecca M. Blank
Acting Secretary of Commerce

cc: Jim Sweetman, Assistant Director, U.S. Government Accountability Office

Appendix VII: GAO Contacts and Staff Acknowledgments

GAO Contacts	David A. Powner, (202) 512-9286 or pownerd@gao.gov Dr. Nabajyoti Barkakati, (202) 512-4499 or barkakatin@gao.gov
Staff Acknowledgments	In addition to the contact names above, individuals making contributions to this report included James R. Sweetman, Jr. (assistant director), Jenny Chanley, Neil Doherty, Rebecca Eyler, Claudia Fletcher, Nancy Glover, and Karl Seifert.

GAO's Mission	The Government Accountability Office, the audit, evaluation, and investigative arm of Congress, exists to support Congress in meeting its constitutional responsibilities and to help improve the performance and accountability of the federal government for the American people. GAO examines the use of public funds; evaluates federal programs and policies; and provides analyses, recommendations, and other assistance to help Congress make informed oversight, policy, and funding decisions. GAO's commitment to good government is reflected in its core values of accountability, integrity, and reliability.
Obtaining Copies of GAO Reports and Testimony	The fastest and easiest way to obtain copies of GAO documents at no cost is through GAO's website (www.gao.gov). Each weekday afternoon, GAO posts on its website newly released reports, testimony, and correspondence. To have GAO e-mail you a list of newly posted products, go to www.gao.gov and select "E-mail Updates."
Order by Phone	The price of each GAO publication reflects GAO's actual cost of production and distribution and depends on the number of pages in the publication and whether the publication is printed in color or black and white. Pricing and ordering information is posted on GAO's website, http://www.gao.gov/ordering.htm. Place orders by calling (202) 512-6000, toll free (866) 801-7077, or TDD (202) 512-2537. Orders may be paid for using American Express, Discover Card, MasterCard, Visa, check, or money order. Call for additional information.
Connect with GAO	Connect with GAO on Facebook, Flickr, Twitter, and YouTube. Subscribe to our RSS Feeds or E-mail Updates. Listen to our Podcasts. Visit GAO on the web at www.gao.gov.
To Report Fraud, Waste, and Abuse in Federal Programs	Contact: Website: www.gao.gov/fraudnet/fraudnet.htm E-mail: fraudnet@gao.gov Automated answering system: (800) 424-5454 or (202) 512-7470
Congressional Relations	Katherine Siggerud, Managing Director, siggerudk@gao.gov, (202) 512-4400, U.S. Government Accountability Office, 441 G Street NW, Room 7125, Washington, DC 20548
Public Affairs	Chuck Young, Managing Director, youngc1@gao.gov, (202) 512-4800 U.S. Government Accountability Office, 441 G Street NW, Room 7149 Washington, DC 20548

Please Print on Recycled Paper.